A grain of mustard-seed: or, the least measure of grace that is or can be effectual to salvation. To which is added some excellent rules of meditation. Corrected and amended by W. Perkins.

William Perkins

A grain of mustard-seed: or, the least measure of grace that is or can be effectual to salvation. To which is added some excellent rules of meditation. Corrected and amended by W. Perkins.
Perkins, William
ESTCID: T203922
Reproduction from British Library
Newcastle : printed and sold by John White, [1750?].
24p. ; 12°

Eighteenth Century
Collections Online
Print Editions

Gale ECCO Print Editions

Relive history with *Eighteenth Century Collections Online*, now available in print for the independent historian and collector. This series includes the most significant English-language and foreign-language works printed in Great Britain during the eighteenth century, and is organized in seven different subject areas including literature and language; medicine, science, and technology; and religion and philosophy. The collection also includes thousands of important works from the Americas.

The eighteenth century has been called "The Age of Enlightenment." It was a period of rapid advance in print culture and publishing, in world exploration, and in the rapid growth of science and technology – all of which had a profound impact on the political and cultural landscape. At the end of the century the American Revolution, French Revolution and Industrial Revolution, perhaps three of the most significant events in modern history, set in motion developments that eventually dominated world political, economic, and social life.

In a groundbreaking effort, Gale initiated a revolution of its own: digitization of epic proportions to preserve these invaluable works in the largest online archive of its kind. Contributions from major world libraries constitute over 175,000 original printed works. Scanned images of the actual pages, rather than transcriptions, recreate the works *as they first appeared.*

Now for the first time, these high-quality digital scans of original works are available via print-on-demand, making them readily accessible to libraries, students, independent scholars, and readers of all ages.

For our initial release we have created seven robust collections to form one the world's most comprehensive catalogs of 18th century works.

Initial Gale ECCO Print Editions collections include:

> ### *History and Geography*
> Rich in titles on English life and social history, this collection spans the world as it was known to eighteenth-century historians and explorers. Titles include a wealth of travel accounts and diaries, histories of nations from throughout the world, and maps and charts of a world that was still being discovered. Students of the War of American Independence will find fascinating accounts from the British side of conflict.

Social Science

Delve into what it was like to live during the eighteenth century by reading the first-hand accounts of everyday people, including city dwellers and farmers, businessmen and bankers, artisans and merchants, artists and their patrons, politicians and their constituents. Original texts make the American, French, and Industrial revolutions vividly contemporary.

Medicine, Science and Technology

Medical theory and practice of the 1700s developed rapidly, as is evidenced by the extensive collection, which includes descriptions of diseases, their conditions, and treatments. Books on science and technology, agriculture, military technology, natural philosophy, even cookbooks, are all contained here.

Literature and Language

Western literary study flows out of eighteenth-century works by Alexander Pope, Daniel Defoe, Henry Fielding, Frances Burney, Denis Diderot, Johann Gottfried Herder, Johann Wolfgang von Goethe, and others. Experience the birth of the modern novel, or compare the development of language using dictionaries and grammar discourses.

Religion and Philosophy

The Age of Enlightenment profoundly enriched religious and philosophical understanding and continues to influence present-day thinking. Works collected here include masterpieces by David Hume, Immanuel Kant, and Jean-Jacques Rousseau, as well as religious sermons and moral debates on the issues of the day, such as the slave trade. The Age of Reason saw conflict between Protestantism and Catholicism transformed into one between faith and logic -- a debate that continues in the twenty-first century.

Law and Reference

This collection reveals the history of English common law and Empire law in a vastly changing world of British expansion. Dominating the legal field is the *Commentaries of the Law of England* by Sir William Blackstone, which first appeared in 1765. Reference works such as almanacs and catalogues continue to educate us by revealing the day-to-day workings of society.

Fine Arts

The eighteenth-century fascination with Greek and Roman antiquity followed the systematic excavation of the ruins at Pompeii and Herculaneum in southern Italy; and after 1750 a neoclassical style dominated all artistic fields. The titles here trace developments in mostly English-language works on painting, sculpture, architecture, music, theater, and other disciplines. Instructional works on musical instruments, catalogs of art objects, comic operas, and more are also included.

The BiblioLife Network

This project was made possible in part by the BiblioLife Network (BLN), a project aimed at addressing some of the huge challenges facing book preservationists around the world. The BLN includes libraries, library networks, archives, subject matter experts, online communities and library service providers. We believe every book ever published should be available as a high-quality print reproduction; printed on-demand anywhere in the world. This insures the ongoing accessibility of the content and helps generate sustainable revenue for the libraries and organizations that work to preserve these important materials.

The following book is in the "public domain" and represents an authentic reproduction of the text as printed by the original publisher. While we have attempted to accurately maintain the integrity of the original work, there are sometimes problems with the original work or the micro-film from which the books were digitized. This can result in minor errors in reproduction. Possible imperfections include missing and blurred pages, poor pictures, markings and other reproduction issues beyond our control. Because this work is culturally important, we have made it available as part of our commitment to protecting, preserving, and promoting the world's literature.

GUIDE TO FOLD-OUTS MAPS and OVERSIZED IMAGES

The book you are reading was digitized from microfilm captured over the past thirty to forty years. Years after the creation of the original microfilm, the book was converted to digital files and made available in an online database.

In an online database, page images do not need to conform to the size restrictions found in a printed book. When converting these images back into a printed bound book, the page sizes are standardized in ways that maintain the detail of the original. For large images, such as fold-out maps, the original page image is split into two or more pages

Guidelines used to determine how to split the page image follows:

• Some images are split vertically; large images require vertical and horizontal splits.
• For horizontal splits, the content is split left to right.
• For vertical splits, the content is split from top to bottom.
• For both vertical and horizontal splits, the image is processed from top left to bottom right.

A
GRAIN
OF
MUSTARD-SEED:

OR, THE

Least Measure of Grace that is or
can be effectual to Salvation.

TO WHICH IS ADDED

Some excellent Rules of Meditation.

Erected and amended by W. PERKINS

MATTH. xvii. 20

*Verily I say unto you, If you have Faith as a Grain
of Mustard seed, ye shall say unto this Mountain
Remove hence to yonder Place, and it shall remove, and nothing shall be impossible unto you*

Newcastle. Printed and sold by JOHN WHITE.

A

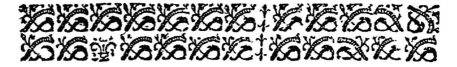

A

GRAIN

OF

MUSTARD SEED, &c.

IT is a very neeeffary Point to be known, *viz*
*What is the leaft Meafure of Grace that can befal
the true Child of God, leffer than which there is no
Grace effectual to Salvation* For *firft*, The Right
underftanding of this, is the very Foundation of true
Comfort unto all troubled and touched Confciences.
Secondly, It is a notable Means to ftir up Thankful-
nefs in them that have any Grace at all; when they
fhall in Examination of hemfelves confider that they
have received of God the leaft Meafure of Grace, or
more. *Thirdly*, It will be an Inducement, and a Spur
unto many carelefs and unrepentant Perfons, to em-
brace the Gofpel, and to begin Repentance for their
Sins, when they fhall perceive, and that by the Word
of God, that God accepts the very Seeds and Rudi-
ments of Faith and Repentance at the firft, though
they be but in a Meafure as a Grain of Muftard feed.

Now then, for the opening and clearing of this
Point, I will fet down fix feveral Conclufions, in
fuch Order as one fhall confirm and explain the other,
and one depend upon the other

CON-

CONCLUSION I.

A Man that doth but begin to be converted, is even at that Inftant the very Child of God, though inwardly he be more Carnal than Spiritual.

The EXPOSITION.

IN a Man there muft be confidered three Things, firft, The Subftance of the Body and Soul, whereof Man is faid to confift, fecondly, The Faculties placed in the Soul and exercifed in the Body, as Underftanding, Will, Affections, and thirdly, The Integrity and Purity of the Faculties, whereby they are conformable to the Will of God, and bear his Image. And fince the Fall of *Adam*, Man is not deprived of his Subftance, or of the Powers and Faculties of his Soul; but only of the third, which is the Purity of Nature And therefore the Converfion of a Sinner, whereof the Conclufion fpeaketh, is not the Change of the Subftance of Man, or the Faculties of the Soul; but a renewing and reftoring of that Purity and Holinefs which was loft by Man's Fall, with the Abolifhment of that natural Corruption that is in all the Powers of the Soul

This is the Work of God only, and on this Manner, *Firft*, When it pleafeth God to work a Change in any, he doth it not firft in one Part and then in another: as he that repairs a decayed Houfe by Piece-meal, but the Work both for the Beginning, Continuance, and Accomplifhment, is in the whole Man, and every Part at one, efpecially in the Mind, Confcience, Will and Affections: As on the Contrary, when *Adam* loft the Image of God, he loft it in every Part, *Secondly,* The

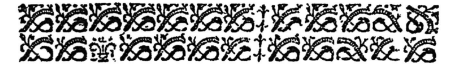

A
GRAIN
OF
MUSTARD SEED, &c.

IT is a very neeeffary Point to be known, *viz*
*What is the leaft Meafure of Grace that can befal
the true Child of God, leffer than which there is no
Grace effectual to Salvation* For *firft*, The Right
underftanding of this, is the very Foundation of true
Comfort unto all troubled and touched Confciences.
Secondly, It is a notable Means to ftir up Thankful-
nefs in them that have any Grace at all; when they
fhall in Examination of hemfelves confider that they
have received of God the leaft Meafure of Grace, or
more. *Thirdly*, It will be an Inducement, and a Spur
unto many carelefs and unrepentant Perfons, to em-
brace the Gofpel, and to begin Repentance for their
Sins, when they fhall perceive, and that by the Word
of God, that God accepts the very Seeds and Rudi-
ments of Faith and Repentance at the firft, though
they be but in a Meafure as a Grain of Muftard feed.

Now then, for the opening and clearing of this
Point, I will fet down fix feveral Conclufions, in
fuch Order as one fhall confirm and explain the other,
and one depend upon the o her.

CON-

CONCLUSION I.

A Man that doth but begin to be converted, is even at that Instant the very Child of God, though inwardly he be more Carnal than Spiritual.

The EXPOSITION

IN a Man there must be considered three Things, first, The Substance of the Body and Soul, whereof Man is said to consist, secondly, The Faculties placed in the Soul and exercised in the Body, as Understanding, Will, Affections, and thirdly, The Integrity and Purity of the Faculties, whereby they are conformable to the Will of God, and bear his Image. And since the Fall of *Adam*, Man is not deprived of his Substance, or of the Powers and Faculties of his Soul; but only of the third, which is the Purity of Nature And therefore the Conversion of a Sinner, whereof the Conclusion speaketh, is not the Change of the Substance of Man, or the Faculties of the Soul; but a renewing and restoring of that Purity and Holiness which was lost by Man's Fall, with the Abolishment of that natural Corruption that is in all the Powers of the Soul

This is the Work of God only, and on this Manner, *First*, When it pleaseth God to work a Change in any, he doth it not first in one Part and then in another: as he that repairs a decayed House by Piece-meal, but the Work both for the Beginning, Continuance, and Accomplishment, is in the whole Man, and every Part at one, especially in the Mind, Conscience, Will and Affections. As on the Contrary, when *Adam* lost the Image of God, he lost it in every Part, *Secondly* The

A 2 Con-

Conversion of a Sinner is not wrought all at one Instant, but in Continuance of Time, and that by certain Measures and Degrees. And a Man is then in the first Degree of his Conversion, when the Holy Ghost by the Means of the Word inspires him with some spiritual Motions, and begins to regenerate and renew the inward Powers of his Soul. And he may in this Case very fitly be compared to the Night in the first Dawning of the Day, in which though the Darkness remain and be more in Quantity than the Light, yet the Sun hath already cast some Beams of Light into the Air, whereupon we term it the Breathing of the Day. Now then, the very Point which I teach is, that a Man at this Instant, and in this very State, (God as yet having but laid certain Beginnings of true Conversion in his Heart) is the very Child of God, and that not only in the eternal Purpose of God, (as all the Elect are) but indeed by actual Adoption, and this is plain by a manifest Reason.

There are four special Works of Grace in every Child of God, *viz.* his Union with Christ, his Adoption, Justification and Conversion; and these four are wrought all at one Instant, so as for Order of Time neither goes before nor after the other. And yet in regard of Order of Nature, Union with Christ, Justification and Adoption, go before the inward Conversion of a Sinner, it being the Fruit and Effect of them all. Upon this it followeth necessarily, that a Sinner in the very first Act of his Conversion, is justified, adopted, and incorporated into the mystical Body of our Lord Jesus Christ.

In the Parable of the Prodigal Son, the Father with Joy receives his wicked Child; but when? Surely when he saw him coming afar off, when as yet he had made no Confession or Humiliation to his Father, but only had conceived with himself a Purpose to return, and to say, *Father, I have sinned against Heaven and in thy Sight, and am no more worthy to be called thy Son* Luke xv. 21. And *Paul* saith of many of the *Corinthians, And I, Brethren, could not*
speak

speak unto you as unto spiritual, but as unto carnal, even as unto Babes in Christ, 1 Cor iii 1 When *David,* reproved by Nathan, did but begin to repent, and to say, *I acknowledge my Sin unto thee,* presently *Nathan* the Prophet of the Lord said, *The Lord hath taken away thy Sin.* Of this Thing *David* seems to speak in the thirty-second *Psalm, I said, that is I purposed and thought with myself, I will confess my Transgressions unto the Lord, and thou forgavest the Iniquity of my Sin.* Psal xxxii 5. Upon these Words *Augustine* saith, *Mark, he doth not confess, but promiseth to confess, and God forgiveth him* And *Ambrose* saith, *If he said I will confess, and obtained Pardon before he confessed, how much more when he had confessed, saying, I know mine Iniquity, was his Sin pardoned* - *Gregory* on this Psalm saith, *Mark how speedily Pardon comes, and how great is the Commendation of God's Mercy, in that Pardon comes together with the Desire of Confession, and Remission comes to the Heart before Confession break forth into Speech.*

CONCLUSION II.

The first material Beginning of the Conversion of a Sinner, or the smallest Measure of renewing Grace, have the Promises of this Life, and that which is to come.

The EXPOSITION

THE Beginnings of Conversion must be distinguish'd Some are Beginnings of Preparation, others are Beginnings of Composition, Beginnings of Preparation are such as bring under, tame and subdue the Stubbornness of Man's Nature, without making any Change at all: Of this Sort are the Accusations

tions of the Conscience by the Ministry of the Law,
Fears and Terrors arising from thence, Compunction
of Heart, which is the Apprehension of God's Anger
against all Sin and Wickedness of what Degree soever.
Now these and the like I exclude in the Conclusion,
for though they go before to prepare a Sinner to his
Conversion following, yet they are not Graces of
God, but Fruits both of the Law, being the Ministry
of Death as also of an accusing Conscience. Beginnings of Composition I call all those inward Motions and Inclinations of God's Spirit, that followeth
after the Work of the Law upon the Conscience,
and rise upon the Meditation of the Gospel, that promises Righteousness and Life everlasting by Christ,
out of which Motions the Conversion of a Sinner
arises: What these are shall afterwards appear

Again, Grace must be distinguished, It is twofold,
restraining Grace, or renewing Grace. Restraining
Grace I call certain common Gifts of God, serving
only to order and frame the outward Conversation
of Men to the Law of God, or serving to bereave
Men of Excuse in the Day of Judgement. By this Sort
of Grace, Heathen Men have been liberal, just, sober,
valiant and merciful By it Men living in the Church
of God have been enlightned, and having tasted of
the good Word of God, have rejoiced therein, and
for a Time outwardly conformed themselves thereto
Renewing-Grace is not common to all Men, but proper to the Elect, and it is a Gift of God's Spirit,
whereby the Corruption of Sin is not only restrained
but also mortified, and the decayed Image of God re-
stored in Righteousness and true Holiness Now then
the Conclusion must only be understood of the se-
cond, and not of the first, for though a Man have
never so much of this restraining Grace, yet, unless
he have the Spirit of Christ to create Faith in the
Heart, and to sanctify him, he is as far from Salvation as any other

Thus then the Sense and Meaning of the Conclusion is, that the very least Measure of saving Grace,
and.

and the very Beginnings or Seeds of Regeneration. do declare, and after a fort, give Title to Men, of all the merciful Promises of God, whether they concern this Life, or that which is to come; and are therefore approved of God if they be in Truth, and accepted as greater Measures of Grace. That which our Saviour Christ faith of the Work of Miracles, *If ye have Faith as a Grain of Mustard feed, ye shall say unto this Mountain, Remove hence to yonder Place, and it shall remove* Matth. xvii 20 must by the Law of equal Proportion be applied to saving Faith, Repentance, the Fear of God, and all other Graces. If they be truly wrought in the Heart, though they be but as small as one little Grain of Mustard feed, they shall be sufficiently effectual to bring forth good Works, for which they are ordained. The Prophet *Isaiah* faith, that *Christ shall not break the bruised Reed. And the smoking Flax shall he not quench*, Isa. xlii 3 Let the Comparison be marked: Fire in Flax must be both little and weak, in Quantity as a Spark or Twain, that cannot cause a Flame, but only a Smoke, especially in a Matter so easy to burn. Here then is signified, that the Gifts and Graces of God's Spirit, that are both for Measure and Strength as a Spark or Twain of Fire, shall not be neglected, but rather accepted and cherished by Christ.

When our Saviour Christ heard the young Man make a Confession of a Practice but of outward and civil Righteousness, *He looked upon him and loved him*, Mark x, 21 And when he heard the Scribe to speak difcreetly but only one good Speech, that to love God with all the Heart is above all Sacrifices, he faid unto him, *That he was not far from the Kingdom of Heaven* Therefore no doubt he will love with a more fpecial Love, and accept as the good Subjects of his Kingdom, those that have received a further Mercy of God, to be born anew of Water and of the Spirit.

A 4 CON-

CONCLUSION III.

A constant and earnest Desire to be reconciled to God, to believe and to repent, if it be in a touched Heart, is in Acceptation with God, as Reconciliation, Faith, Repentance itself.

The EXPOSITION.

LUST or Desire is twofold, natural and supernatural. Natural Desire is that whose Beginning and Object is in Nature, that is, which arises of the natural Will of Man, and affecteth such Things as are thought to be good according to the Light of Nature. And this kind of Desire hath its Degrees, yet so as they are all limited within the Compass of Nature. Some desire Riches, Honours and Pleasures, some Learning and Knowledge, because it is the Light and Perfection of the Mind: Some go further and seek after the Virtues of Justice, Temperance, Liberality, &c. and thus many Heathen Men have excelled. Some again desire true Happiness, as *Balaam* did, who wished to die the Death of the Righteous, because it is the Property of Nature to seek the Preservation of itself. But here Nature stays herself, for where the Mind reveals not the Will affects not.

Supernatural Desires are such as both for their Beginning and Object are above Nature. For their Beginning is from the Holy Ghost, and the Object or Matter about which they are conversant, are Things divine and spiritual, which concern the Kingdom of Heaven: And of this Kind are the Desires of which I speak in this Place.

Again, that we may not be deceived in our Desires, but may the better discern them from fluttering and fleeting Motions, I add three Restraints. *First*, The
Desire

Defire of Reconciliation; the Defire to believe, or the Defire to repent, &c, muft be conftant, and have Continuance, otherwife it may juftly be fufpected. Secondly, It muft be earneft and ferious, though not always, yet at fometimes, that we may be able to fay; with *David, My Soul defireth after thee, O Lord, as the thirfty Land. And as the Hart brayeth after the Rivers of Water, fo panteth my Soul after thee, O God, My Soul thirfteth for God, even the Living God,* Pfal. xlii. 1, 2. Thirdly, it muft be in a touched heart; for when a Man is touched in Confcience, the Heart is caft down, and (as much as it can) it withdraws itfelf from God: For this Caufe, if then there be any fpiritual Motions whereby the Heart is lift up unto God they are without doubt from the Spirit of God. Thus then I avouch, that the Defire of Reconciliation with God in Chrift, is Reconciliation itfelf: The Defire to believe is Faith indeed, and the Defire to repent, Repentance itfelf: But mark how: A Defire to be reconciled, is not Reconciliation in Nature, (for, the Defire is one Thing, and Reconciliation is another) but in God's Acceptation: For if we, being touched throughly for our Sins, do defire to have them pardoned, and to be at one with God, God accepts us as reconciled Again Defire to believe, it is not Faith in Nature but only in God's Acceptation, God accepting the Will for the Deed.

That this Doctrine is the Will and Word of God, it appears by thefe Reafons First, God hath annexed a Promife of Bleffednefs, and of Life everlafting to the Defire of Grace. *Bleffed are they which do hunger and thirst after Righteoufnefs For they shall be filled.* Matth v 6 *If any Man thirst, let him come unto me and thirst,* John vii 37 *I will give unto him that is a thirst, of the Fountain of the Water of Life freely,* Rev. xx 6 Now, what is this to thirst? Properly it is when we are in a Drought or Drinefs, and want Drink to refresh us, to defire it. And therefore by all Refemblance, they are faid to thirst after Righteoufnefs that want it, and would fain have it: And they thirst after

after Chrift, that feel themfelves out of Chrift, and
defire, yea, long after the Blood of Chrift, that they
might be refrefhed with it in their Confciences Here
then we fee, that the Defire of Mercy, in the Want
of Mercy, is the obtaining of Mercy, and the Defire
to believe in the Want of Faith' is Faith. Remember then, though as yet thou want firm and lively
Grace, yet art thou not altogether void of Grace: If
thou canft unfeignedly defire it, thy Defire is the Seed,
Conception, or Bud, of that which thou winneft.
Now is the Spring-time of the ingrafted Word, or
the immortal Seed caft into the Furrows of thy Heart.
Wait but a While, ufing the good Means to this End
appointed, and thou fhalt fee the Leaves, Bloffoms,
and Fruit will foon follow af er

Secondly, The Defire of any good Thing is accepted
of God as the lively Invocation of his holy Name,
God heareth the Defires of the Poor, Pfal x 17 *He
will fulfil the Defire of them that fear him,* Pfal cxlv. 19.
When *Mofes* faid nothing, but only defired in Heart
the Help and Protection of God at the Red Sea, *The
Lord faid urto him, Wherefore crieft thou unto me?* Exod.
xiv. 15 *And when we know not to pray as we ought,
Paul* faith, *that the Spirt maketh Requeft by the inward
Groans of the Heart,* Rom viii 26.

Hence I gather, that when a Man in his Weaknefs
prays with Sighs and Groans for the Gift of lively
Faith, the Want whereof he finds in himfelf, his very
Prayer on this Manner made, is as truly in Acceptation with God as this Prayer made in lively Faith It
is further to be confidered here, that *Paul* calls thefe
Groans unfpeakable, and why? Of moft Interpreters
they are thought to be unfpeakable becaufe of their
Greatnefs, and this I will not deny. It feems never-
thelefs that they are fo called by reafon of their Weaknefs, for they are commonly fmall, weak, and con-
fufed in the Hearts of God's Children when they are
diftreffed; and the Words following feem to import
thus much · For when it had been faid that God's Spirit in us makes Requeft with Groans not to be uttered,

                                        fome

some Men might happily reply and say, if we cannot
discern and utter these Groans in ourselves, what are
we the better? *Paul* adds therefore, that altogether we
know not, yet God, a Searcher of all Things hidden
in the Heart, knows the Mind and Meaning of the
Spirit.   And thus the Words yet further afford a com-
fortable Instruction to the Children of God, namely,
that being in Distress, whether in Life or Death, if
by Grace we can but sigh or sob unto God, though it
be weak and feeble like the faint Pulse in the Time
of Death, we, or the Spirit of God in us, do indeed
make Request unto God that shall be heard, yea, (as
the Words are) we do more than make Requests:
And although we do not always see what God's Spirit
makes us to sigh after, yet God doth.
    Thirdly, To the Testimony of Scripture I add the
Testimonies of godly learned Men, not to prove
the Doctrine in Hand, but to shew a Consent, and to
prove thus much, that the Thing which I avouch is
no private Phantasy of any Man. *Augustin* saith, *Let
thy Desire be before him, and thy Father which seeth in
secret shall reward thee openly. For thy Desire is thy
Prayer; and if thy Desire be continual, thy Prayer is
continual* He adds further, *that the Desire is a continual Voice, and the Cry of the Heart, and the inward
Invocation of God, which may be without Intermission.*
Again, *To edify the Help of Grace, is the Beginning of
Grace.* Again, *The whole Life of a good Christian is an
holy Will and Desire: And that which indeed thou
desirest, thou see'st not, but by desiring, art as it were
enlarged and made capable, that when it shall come
which thou shalt see, thou must be filled.* *Basil* saith,
Thou must will, and God will come of his own Accord.
Bernard saith, *What, is not Desire a Voice? Yea, a very
strong Voice God heareth the Desire of the Poor; and
a continual Desire, though we speak nothing, is a Voice
continued* *Luther* saith, *Christ is then truly omnipo-
tent, and then truly reigns in us, when we are so weak
that we can scarce give any Groan For Paul saith, that
one such Groan is a strong Cry in the Ears of God, filling*
                                           both.

both Heaven and Earth Again, Very few know how weak and small Faith and Hope is under the Cross and Temptation; for it appears then to be as smoaking Flax, which a good Blast of Wind would presently put out; But such as believe in those Combats and Terrors, against Hope under Hope, that is opposing themselves by Faith in the Promise of Christ, against the feeling of Sin, and the Wrath of God, do find afterwards that this little spark of Faith (as it appears to Reason, which hardly perceiveth it) is peradventure as the whole Element of Fire, which filleth all Heaven, and swalloweth up all Terrors and Sins. Again, The more we find our Unworthiness, and the less we find the Promise to belong to us, the more must we desire them; being assured that this Desire doth greatly please God, who desireth and willeth that his Grace should be earnestly desired. This doth Faith, which judgeth it a precious Thing, and therefore greatly hungereth and thirsteth after it, and so obtains it For God is delighted to fill the Hungry with good Things, and to send the Rich empty away Theodore Beza saith, if thou find not thine Heart inwardly touched, pray that it may be touched. For then must thou know that this Desire is a Pledge of the Father's Good-will to thee. Kemnitius saith, When I have a good Desire, though it do scarcely shew itself in some little and slender Sigh, I must be assured that the Spirit of God is present, and worketh his good Work. Urfinus saith, Faith in the most holy Men in this Life is imperfect and weak · Yet nevertheless, whosoever feels in his Heart an earnest Desire to believe, and a striving against his natural Doubtings both can and must assure himself that he is endued with true Faith Again, Wicked Men do not desire the Grace of the Holy Spirit, whereby they may resist Sin, and therefore they are justly deprived of it · For he that earnestly desireth the Holy Ghost, hath it already; because this Desire of the Spirit cannot be but from the Spirit. As it is said, Blessed are they that hunger and thirst after Righteousness, for they shall be satisfied. Bradford saith, Thy Sins are undoubtedly pardoned, &c. for God hath given thee a penitent and believing Heart, that is,

an

an *Heart which defireth to repent and believe*· For fuch
an one is taken of him (he accepting the Will for the
Deed, for a penitent and believing Heart *Taffin* faith,
Our Faith may be fo fmall and weak, as it doth not yet
bring forth Fruits that may be lively felt of us, but if
they which feel themfelves in fuch a State defire to have
thefe Feelings, (namely of God's Favour and Love) if
they ask them at God's Hands by Prayer, this Defire
and Prayer are Teftimonies that the Spirit of God is in
them, And that they have Faith already: For, is fuch
a Defire a Fruit of the Flefh, or of the Spirit? It is of
the Holy Spirit, who bringeth it forth only in fuch as he
dwells in, &c Then thefe holy Defires and Prayers being the Motions of the Holy Ghoft in us, are Teftimonies
of our Faith, although they feem to us fmall and weak
As the Woman that feeleth the Moving of a Child in her
Body, though very weak, affureth herfelf that fhe hath
conceived. and that fhe goeth with a live Child So if
we have thefe Motions, thefe holy Affections and Defires
before mentioned, let us not doubt but that we have the
Holy Ghoft, who is the Author of them, dwelling in us,
and confequently that we have alfo Faith. Again, he
faith, 1ft, If thou haft begun to hate and flie fin, 2dly
If thou feeleft that thou art difpleafed in thine Infirmi-
ties and Corruptions, 3dly, If having offended God thou
feeleft a Grief, and a Sorrow for it, 4thly, If thou defires to abftain, 5thly. If thou avoideft the Occafions;
6thly, If thou travelleft to do thy Endeavour; 7thly, If
thou prayeft to God to give thee Grace. All thefe holy
Affections, proceeding from none other than the Spirit of
God, ought to be fo many Pledges and Teftimonies that
he is in thee. Mr Knox faith, Albeit your Pains fometimes be fo horrible that you find no Releafe nor Comfort,
neither in Spirit nor Body; yet if thy Heart can only fob
unto God, defpair not, you fhall obtain your Heart's Defire, and you are not deftitute of Faith. For at fuch
Time as the Flefh, natural Reafon, the Law of God, the
prefent Torment, the Devil as one do Cry, God is angry,
and therefore there is neither Help nor Remedy to be hoped
for at his Hands: At fuch a Time, I fay, to fob unto
God,

God, is the Demonſtration of the ſecret Seed of God, which is hid in God's elect Children, and that only Sob is unto God a moſt acceptable Sacrifice, than without this Croſs to give our Bodies to be burnt even for the Truth's Sake. Theſe Teſtimonies will I hope ſuffice

Againſt this Points of Doctrine it may be alledged, That, if Deſire to believe in our Weakneſs be Faith indeed, then ſome are juſtified, and may be ſaved wanting a lively Apprehenſion and full Perſuaſion of God's Mercy in Chriſt. *Anſwer,* Juſtifying Faith in regard of his Nature, is always the ſame; and the eſſential Property thereof is to apprehend Chriſt and his Benefits, and to aſſure the very Conſcience thereof And therefore without ſome Apprehenſion and Aſſurance, there can be no Juſtification or Salvation in them that for Age are able to believe Yet there be certain Degrees and Meaſures of true Faith. There is a ſtrong Faith, which cauſes a full Apprehenſion and Perſuaſion of God's Mercy in Chriſt. This Meaſure of Faith the Lord vouchſafed *Abraham, David, Paul,* the Prophets, Apoſtles, and Martyrs of God. It were a bleſſed Thing, if all Believers might attain to this Height of lively Faith, to ſay with *Paul,* I am perſuaded, that *neither Life, nor Death, nor any Thing elſe, ſhall be able to ſeperate us from the Love of God in Chriſt.* But all cannot. Therefore there is another Degree of Faith lower than the former and yet true Faith, *viz* little or great Faith; and it alſo hath Power to apprehend and apply the Promiſe of Salvation, but as yet, by reaſon of Weakneſs, it is unfolded as it were, and wrapt up in the Heart, as the Leaf and Bloſſom in the Bud. For ſuch Perſons as have this weak Faith, can ſay that they believe their Sins to be pardonable, and that they deſire to have them pardoned; but as yet cannot ſay that they are pardoned. And yet the Mercy of God is not wanting unto them. For in that they do and can deſire, and endeavour to apprehend, they do indeed apprehend; God accepting the Deſire to do the Thing for the Thing done This which I ſay will the better appear if the Grounds thereof

thereof be confidered   Faith doeft not juftify in refpect of itfelf, becaufe it is an Action of Virtue, or
becaufe it is ftrong, lively and perfect, but in refpect
of the Object thereof, namely, Chrift crucified, whom
Faith apprehendeth as he is fet forth unto us in the
Word and Sacraments.   Is it Chrift that is the Author and Matter of our Juftice, and it is he that ap-
plieth the fame unto us: As for Faith in us, it is but
an Inftrument to apprehend and receive that which
Chrift for his Part offereth and giveth.   Therefore,
if Faith err not in his proper Object, but follow the
Promife of God, though it do weekly apprehend, or
at the leaft caufe a Man only to endeavour and defire to apprehend it, it is true Faith, and juftifieth.
Though our Apprehenfion be neceffary, yet our Salvation ftands rather in this, that God apprehends us
for his own, than that we apprehend him, *Phil.* iii   12.
And rather in this, that we are known of him, than
that we know him, *Gal.* iv   9
   Out of this Conclufion fprings another, not to be
omitted, *That God accepts the Endeavour of the whole
Man to obey, for perfect Obedience itfelf.*   That is, if
Men endeavour to pleafe God in all Things, God
will not judge their doing by the Rigour of his Law,
but will accept their little and weak Endeavour, to
do that which they can do by his Grace, as if they
had perfectly fulfilled the Law.   But here remember
I put in this Caveat, that this Endeavour muft be in and
by the whole Man; the very Mind, Confcience, Will
and Affections, doing that which they can in their
Kinds: And thus the Endeavour to obey, which is a
Fruit of the Spirit, fhall be diftinguifhed from civil
Righteoufnefs, which may be in Heathen Man, and
is only in the outward and not in the inward Man.
   The Truth of this Conclufion appears by that which
the Prophet *Malachi* faith, that God will fpare them
that fear him, *as a Father fpares his Child,* Mal. iii   17.
who accepts the Thing done as welcome, if the Child
fhew his Good-will to pleafe his Father, and to do
what he can.

CON-

CONCLUSION IV.

To see and feel in ourselves the Want of any Grace pertaineth to Salvation, and to be grieved, therefore, is the Grace itself

The EXPOSITION.

UNDERSTAND this Conclusion as the former, namely, that Grief of Heart for the Want of any Grace necessary to Salvation, is as much with God as the Grace itself. When being in Distress we cannot pray as we ought, God accepts the very Groans, Sobs, and Sighs of the perplexed Heart as the Prayer itself, *Rom.* viii. 26. When we are grieved because we cannot be grieved for our Sins, it is a Degree and Measure of godly Sorrow, before God.

Augustine saith well, *Sometimes our Prayer is lukewarm, or rather cold, and almost no Prayer, nay, sometimes it is altogether no Prayer at all, and yet we cannot with Grief perceive this in ourselves·* For if we can but grieve because we cannot pray, we now pray indeed. *Hiram* saith, *Then we are just when we acknowledge ourselves to be Sinners.* Again, *This is the true Wisdom of Man, to know himself to be imperfect.* And (that I may so speak) *the Perfection of all just Men in the Flesh is imperfect. Augustin* again saith, *That the Virtue which is now in a just Man is thus far perfect, that unto the Perfection thereof there belongs a true Acknowledgement and an humble Confession of the Imperfection thereof.* A broken and contrite Heart after an Offence, is as much with God as if there had been no Offence at all. And therefore as soon as *David* after his grievous Fall, in Heaviness of Heart confessed his Sin, saying in Effect but thus much, *I have sinned*, the Prophet in
th

the Name of the Lord pronounceth the Pardon o
Sin in Heaven, and that presently.

CONCLUSION V.

*He that hath begun to subject himself to Christ
and his Word, though as yet he be ignorant
in most Points of Religion, yet if he have a
Care to encrease in Knowledge, and to practise
that which he knoweth, he is accepted of God as
a true Believer.*

The EXPOSITION.

SUNDRY Persons by the Evangelists are said to
believe, which had only seen the Miracles of Jesus Christ, and as yet had made no further Proceeding, but to acknowledge Christ to be the Messias,
and to submit themselves to him and his Doctrine,
which afterwards should be taught. On this Manner
the Woman of *Samaria* believed, and many of the
Samaritans upon her Report. And a certain Ruler, by
Reason of a Miracle wrought upon his Son, is said to
believe, and all his Houshold, *John* iv. 42, 53.

When our Saviour Christ commendeth the Faith of
the Apostles, calling it a Rock, against which the
Gates of Hell should not prevail, it was not for the
plentiful Knowledge of the Doctrine of Salvation, for
they were ignorant of many Articles of Faith, as the
Death, Resurrection, Ascension, and Kingdom of
Christ, but because they believed him to be the Son
of God, and the Saviour of Mankind, and they had
withal resolved themselves to cleave unto Him, and
the blessed Doctrine of Salvation which he taught,
though as yet they were ignorant in many Points.
The Holy Ghost commendeth the Faith of *Rahab*,
when she received the Spies. Now this her Faith was
indeed

Indeed but a Seed and Beginning of lively Faith: For then she had only heard of the Miracles done in *E-gypt*, and of the Deliverance of the *Israelites*, and was thereupon smitten with a Fear, and had conceived a Resolution with herself to join herself to the *Israelite*, and to worship the true God.

Now these and the like are called Believers upon just Cause, for though they be ignorant as yet, yet their Ignorance shall be no continuing or lasting Ignorance: And they have excellent Seeds of Grace, namely, a Purpose of Heart to cleave to Christ; and a Care to profit in the Doctrine of Salvation.

CONCLUSION VI.

The foresaid Beginnings of Grace are counterfeit, unless they encrease.

The EXPOSITION.

THE Wickedness of Man's Nature, and the Depth of Hypocrisy are such, that a Man may and can easily transform himself into the Counterfeit and Resemblance of any Grace of God Therefore I put down here a certain Note whereby the Gifts of God may be discerned, namely, that they grow up and encrease as the Grain of Mustard-seed to a great Tree, and bear Fruit answerably The Grace in the Heart is like the Grain of Mustard-seed in two Things; first, It is small to see to at the Beginning; secondly, After it is cast into the Ground of the Heart, it encreaseth speedily, and spreads itself. Therefore, if a Man at the first have but some little Feeling of his Wants, some weak and faint Desire, some small Obedience, he must not let this Spark of Grace go out, but these Motions of the Spirit must be encreased by the Use of the Words Sacraments and Prayer; and they must

daily

daily be ftirred up by meditation, endeavouring, ftriving, afking, feeking, knocking. The Mafter delivering his Talents to his Servants, faith unto them, *Occupy 'till I come,* and not hide them in the Earth, *Matth.* xxu, 25 *Paul* ufeth an excellent Speech to *Timothy.* I exhort thee to ftir up the Gift of God which is in thee, namely, as Fire is ftirred up by often blowing, and putting to of Wood 2 *T.m* 1, 6. As for fuch Motions of the Heart that laft for a Week, or a Month, and after vanifh away, they are not to be regarded, And the Lord by the Prophet complaineth of them: faying, O *Ephrair, thy Righteoufnefs is like the Morning Dew,* Hof vi, 4

Therefore confidering Grace unlefs it be confirmed and exercifed, is indeed no Grace I will here add certain Rules of Direction, that we may the more eafily put in Practice the fpiritual Exercifes of Invocation, Faith and Repentance; and thereby alfo quicken and revive the Seeds and Beginnings of Grace.

1 In what Place foever thou art, whether alone or abroad, by Day or by Night, and whatfoever thou art doing, fet thyfelf in the Prefence of God : Let this Perfuafion always take Place in thy Heart, that thou art before the living God, and do thy Endeavour that this Perfuafion may fmite thy Heart with Awe and Reverence, and make thee afraid to fin This Counfel the Lord gave *Abraham, Walk before me, and be thou perfect.* This Thing alfo was practifed by *Enoch,* who for this Cafe is faid to walk with God

2 Efteem of every prefent Day as of the Day of thy Death. And therefore live as though thou were dying, and do thofe good Duties every Day that thou wouldft do if thou were dying: This is Chriftian Watchfulnefs, and remember it.

2, Make Catalogues and Bills of thine own Sins, efpecially of thofe Sins that have moft difhonoured God, and wounded thine own Confcience : Set them before thee often, efpecially when thou haft any particular Occafion of renewing thy Repentance; that thy Heart by this doleful Sight, may be further hum-

bled. This was *David*'s Practice, when he considered
his Ways, and turned his Feet unto God's Commandments, *Psal* cxix 59 And when he confessed the
Sins of his Youth, *Psal.* xxv 7 This was *Job*'s Practice, when he said he was not able to answer one of
a Thousand of his Sins unto God, *Job* ix 3

4. When thou first openest thine Eyes in a Morning, pray to God, and give him Thanks heartily: God
then shall have his Honour, and thy Heart shall be
the better for it the whole Day following, for we see
in Experience, that Vessels keep long the Taste of
that Liquor wherewith they are first season'd And
when thou liest down let that be the last also. for
thou knowest not, when once thou art fallen asleep,
whether thou shalt ever rise again alive Good therefore it is, that thou shouldst give up thyself into the
Hands of God, whilst thou art waking

5 Labour to see and feel thy spiritual Poverty, that
is, to see the Want of Grace in thyself, especially
those inward Corruptions of Unbelief, Pride, Self-
love, &c Labour to be displeased with thyself, and
labour to feel that by Reason of them, thou standest
in Need of every Drop of the Blood of Christ to heal
and cleanse thee from these Wants. And let this Practice take such Place with thee, that if thou be asked,
what in thine Estimation is the vilest of the Creatures
upon Earth? Thine Heart and Conscience may an-
wer with a loud Voice, *I, even I, by reason of mine
own Sins.* And again, if thou be asked, what is the
best Thing in the World for thee? Thy Heart and
Conscience may answer again with a strong and loud
Cry, *One Drop of the Blood of Christ to wash away my
Sins*

6. Shew thyself to be a Member of Christ, and a
Servant of God, not only in the general Calling of a
Christian, but also in the particular Calling in which
thou art placed It is not enough for a Magistrate
to be a Christian Man, but he must also be a Christian Magistrate. It is not enough for a Master of a
Family to be a Christian Man, or a Christian in the

Church

Church, but he must also be a Christian in his Family, and in the Trade which he followeth daily   Not every one that is a common Hearer of the Word, and a Frequenter of the Lord's Table, is therefore a good Christian unless his Conversation in his private House, and in his private Affairs and Dealings be suitable   There is a Man to be seen what he is

7 Search the Scriptures, to see what is Sin, and what is not Sin in every Action: This done, carry in thy Heart a constant and resolute Purpose not to sin in any Thing. for Faith and the Purpose of Sinning can never stand together

8 Let thine Endeavour be suitable to thy Purpose; and therefore do nothing at any Time against thy Conscience, rightly inform'd by the Word: Exercise thyself to eschew every Sin, and to obey God in every one of his Commandments, that pertain either to the general Calling of a Christian, or to thy particular Calling   Thus did good *Josias*, who turned unto God with all his Heart, according to all the Law of *Moses*   And thus did *Zacharriah* and *Elizabeth* that walked in all the Commandments of God without Reproof, *Luke* 1 6.

9 If at any Time against thy Purpose and Resolution, thou be overtaken with any Sin little or great, lie not in it, but speedily recover thyself by Repentance · Humble thyself, confessing thine Offence, and by Prayer entreating the Lord to pardon the same, and that earnestly, till such Time as thou findest thy Conscience truly pacified, and thy Care to eschew the same Sin encreased

10 Consider of the right and proper End of thy Life in this World, which is not to seek Profit, Honour, Pleasure, but that in serving of Men we might serve God in our Callings. God could, if it so pleased him, preserve Man without the Ministry of Man; but his Pleasure is to fulfil his Work and Will in the Preservation of our Bodies and Salvation of our Souls, by the Employment of Men in his Service, every one according to his Vocation ; Neither is there so much

as

as a bond Slave, but he muſt in and by his faithful
Service to his Maſter, ſerve the Lord. Men therefore
do commonly profane their Labours and Lives, by
aiming at a wrong End, when all their Care conſiſt-
eth only in getting ſufficient Maintenance for them
and theirs, for the obtaining o Credit, Riches, and
carnal Commodities For thus Men ſerve themſelves,
and not God or Men, much leſs do they ſerve God
in ſerving of Men

11 Give all Diligence to make thy Election ſure,
and to gather manifold Tokens thereof For this
Cauſe obſerve the Works of God's Providence, Love
and Mercy, both in thee and upon thee from Time
to Time For the ſerious Conſideration of them, and
the laying of them together when they are many and
ſeveral, miniſter much Direction, Aſſurance of God's
Favour and Comfort This was the Practice of *David*, 1 *Sam*. XVII. 33 *Pſal*. XXIII.

12. Think evermore thy preſent Eſtate, whatſoever
it be, to be the beſt Eſtate for thee, becauſe whatſoever befals thee though it be Sickneſs, any other Af-
fliction, or Death, 'tis the good Providence of God.
That this may the better be done, labour to ſee and
acknowledge God's Providence, as well as in Poverty
as in Plenty, in Diſgrace as good Report, in Sickneſs
as in Health, and in Life as in Death.

13. Pray continually, I mean not by ſolemn and ſet
Prayer, but by ſecret and inward Ejaculations of the
Heart, that is, by a continual Elevation of Mind unto Chriſt, ſitting at the Right Hand of God the Father,
and that either by Prayer or giving of Thanks ſo
often as Occaſion ſhall offer.

14. Think often of the worſt and moſt grievous
Things that may befal thee either in Life or Death
for the Name of Chriſt Make a Reckoning of them,
and prepare thyſelf to bear them that when they come
they may not ſeem ſtrange, and be born eaſily.

15. Make Conſcience of idle, vain, diſhoneſt, and
ungodly Thoughts; for theſe are the Seeds and Beginnings of actual Sin in Word and Deed. This Want

of Care in ordering and compoſing of our Thoughts, is often puniſhed with a fearful Temptation in the very Thonght, called of Divines a Temptation of Blaſphemies.

16 When any good Motion or Affection riſeth in the Heart, ſuffer it not to paſs away, but feed it by Reading, Meditation and Prayer.

17. Whatſoever good Thing thou goeſt about, whether it be in Word or Deed, do it not in a Conceit of thyſelf, or in the Pride of thy Heart, but in Humility, aſcribing the Power whereby thou doeſt thy Work, and the Praiſe thereof to God, otherwiſe thou ſhalt find by Experience God will curſe thy beſt Doings.

18 Deſpiſe not civil Honeſty; good Conſcience and good Manners muſt go together: Therefore remember to make Conſcience of Lying and cuſtomable Swearing in common Talk. Contend not either in Deed or Word with any Man, be courteous and gentle to all, good and bad: Bear with Mens Wants and Frailties, as Haſtineſs, Forwardneſs, Self-liking, Curiouſneſs, &c paſſing by them as being not perceived: Return not Evil for Evil, but rather Good for Evil: Uſe Meat, Drink and Apparel in that Manner and Meaſure, that they may further Godlineſs, and may be as it were Signs in which thou may'ſt expreſs the hidden Grace of thy Heart: Strive not to go beyond any unleſs it be in good Things: Go before thine Equals in giving of Honour, rather than in taking of it: Make Conſcience of thy Word, and let it be as a Bond. Profeſs not more outwardly than thou haſt inwardly in Heart: Oppreſs or defraud no Man in Bargaining; and in all Companies either do Good, or take Good.

19 Cleave not by inordinate Affection to any Creature; but above all Things quiet and reſt thy Mind in Chriſt; above all Dignity and Honour, above all Cunning and Policy, above all Glory and Honour, above all Health and Beauty, above all Wealth and Treaſure; above all Joy and Delight, above all Fame and
Praiſe,

Praise, and above all Mirth and Consolation, that Man's Heart can feel or devise beside Christ.

✻✻✻✻✻✻✻✻✻✻✻✻✻✻✻✻✻✻✻✻✻✻✻✻✻

The following excellent Rules of Meditation I pro-
pound unto thee, as I find them laid down by Vic-
torinus Strigelius, a learned Divine.

I. WE must not turn away from God for any Creature.

II. Infinite Eternity is ever to be preferred before
the short Race of this mortal Life.

III. We must hold fast the Promise of Grace, though
we lose all temporal Blessings, and they also in Death
must needs be lost.

IV. Let the Love of God in Christ, and the Love
of the Church for Christ, be stronger in thee, and prevail against all other Affections.

V. It is the principal Art of a Christian to believe
Things invisible, to hope for Things deferred, to love
God when he shews him to be an Enemy, and that
to persevere unto the End.

VI. It is most effectual Remedy for any Grief
to quiet ourselves in a Confidence of the Presence and
Help of God, and to ask of him, and withal to wait
either for some Easement or Deliverance.

VII. All the Works of God are done in contrary
Means.

FINIS.

CPSIA information can be obtained at www.ICGtesting.com
Printed in the USA
BVOW04s0822220416

445235BV00009B/52/P